TO YOU FROM YOU V

TO YOU FROM YOU V

FARAH ALQATTAN

Copyright @ 2024 by Farah Alqattan
www.farahalqattan.com

All rights reserved.

No part of this book may be reproduced whatsoever,
without written permission except in the case of brief quotations
embodied in articles and reviews.

Print Version 1: September, 2024
Print ISBN: 979-8-9881785-5-2
Library of Congress Control Number: 2024922275
For permission requests, contact: Support@farahalqattan.com
Author Instagram: farahalqattanofficial
Publisher Instagram: Rwhpublishing
Author Website: www.farahalqattan.com

Rwh Publishing LLC produces creative content by artists who aim to
uplift humanity and change lives for the better.

Table of Contents

Orbit
Fulfill
Clover Field
Pro Bono
Ad Sum
Amal
Universal Foul Call
Hydraulics
Bind
Emocurruncy
Slide Tides
Realize
Bold Action
Stimulant
Fracking Quackery
Jayed
The Upright Don't Fight
Superb Symphony
Beyond the Veil
Index Record
Companion
Originality
Hero Win

Act with love, Better Help
Blueberry Muffin
Sweet Honeycomb
Bonjur
Better Belief
Relief
Huey of Que Heuristics
Lucky Gem
Goldhood Robinhood
Taxonomy Mommy
Harmlytics
Positive Force
Twin Power
Orchid Paradise
Hood Mysteries
En Banc Review
Justice League
New Path

Orbit

The true one
Under the tree
Who here is able to see?

Those walking in
To be fed
And later return

At the corner, under a structure
A foundation of truth shelter

The ones making ends meet
Without hate into others near
Growing awareness

The ones or the one
Here
The becoming

Unity lighthouses

Fulfill

Put your handout
Put it out
Into the open
Just for this moment

Hold your hand out
-pause and look-
Feel love pouring into your orbit

Breathe it

Keep holding your hand out for me
Anytime anger or frustrations surfaces

Here, extend it farther out
Feel now
A bigger embrace around you

Did you do it?
Try it again
Gaze

Perception can be shaped to harm you
Or like this, can uplift and love you

Be aware friend, love will feel different
Do it outside in the sun on your walk
And remember these words,
'This love outlasts'

Your inner being may tremble
But it's only because love is powerful

It won't give up on you
Not at your lowest
Even when you're the greatest

It fills you up
Without materials or cravings
Pours into your cup
Soul richness

Faithfulness
Never give up on us
Not in spirit essence
We have won the wars

Even if tears stream
New oceans and currents, rivers
No bias
It's not all about the climate changes
Perhaps the little wins
Like this

Clover Field

As you walk
Each step
Opens a doorway

So where can courage take us?
Perhaps, brimming
Up above

Will leading through the uncharted
Into new perception
Open horizons
Into a new dawn
Away from the darkness
Changing standards
Leaning into true leadership
A vision

Pro Bono

Justice
And the laws
Have you read through them all?
To grow in awareness

Not in applicability or enforcement
But think backwards

If a statute is derived from passion
How insightful are we to understand the power of emotions

If the law is against carelessness
Why do we implement that which breeds it?

If taking a life is murder
What has been derived leading to extinction?

What will we do?
How will each think?
To reach wisdom ways

What have we designed?
What has been stimulated?
Who can see beyond the chaotic?

Chromatic
Not a honey pot
Something more golden

Ad Sum

You can walk in dullness
Full of thought
'How could I have done that to the ones I love'

Understanding capability is important
Perhaps it's the experience of authenticity spurring humility

Don't ruminate long
Trust the unseen,
deriving better solutions

Sharing the goodness in the guidance
Reminding others,
"you can choose peacefulness and lead with love out in the open"

What will become of us, should we choose?
A new purpose vision
Trust of fortunes

Amal

It is an angel
Or is it religion?
Is it party lines?
Or a collective

How can one transcend?
Beyond the fighting
Sitting in stillness

Seeing the other just as worthy
Beyond wrongs or rights
Beyond hurt manifestations
Inspired to ask better questions

In love sharing
Pouring
Truth understanding and opportunities
Support of character development

It's true
Covering with healing
To lift, beyond hurts
To see souls glowing

Can you see their frowns turn to smiles?
Beam from the inside-out like new children
It's possible
To turn a dark page to a new canvas
Full of bright colors
Lighthouses

Universal Foul Call

Fighting in a cage
Is that soul expression?
Is it for love?
Or perhaps profit

Who is using the souls
To make fortunes
While they call it sports

Who has allowed, the souls to go about hurting each other?
Do they not know, what is written?

Why popularize the hurt?
Paper-view
Is it the truth?

The need to release aggression is evident
There are other ways
Perhaps calisthenics
Building new family shelters
Leaning on spirit understanding

Will those who fight
Have to go back home to their little ones
That will witness them
Then in generations, mimic them
Repeating the cycle

Or will each have it in them
To change history, to love and cultivate peacefulness

Hydraulics

Every color on the spectrum
But what about the state
Water or ice cubes
How can heat dissolve you?
Even through evaporation
Can each bring about,
water to nourish and clean
Through kind expression with understanding here
Hear

Let this serve all who need it, to be uplifted
Fill their well up with new fortunes
Deeper understanding

Pouring into the hearts of those near
Its beautiful when we think different
Perhaps changing from hurt outcomes
Giving a new mindset,
that takes beyond the horizons

Sharing truth gems
Alternate perspective
As a new solution to existing problems

Yes, it's known
There are those who still operate
But what about the story?
Isn't an opportunity?

Can we believe in the overcoming?
To notice, those who fell are now soaring

Understanding
All is possible
Beyond the clusters
Filibuster
As long as, we don't give up on each other

Aiming to lead with kindness
Perhaps gentleness can better serve us
On the cheeks, of those near
A smile so sincere
Can be seen
The radiance
Glowing from within
It's within you as well
Rather than frowns
That rob us blind
In hospitals from depression

Glimmers of soft eyes
Seek to lift not harm
Oh sweet one, love gives more fortune

Bind

She didn't do it for the Palestinians
Though they will be freed
And those who harmed them build them castles

She's doing it for the veterans she spoke with
While working in customer service
The veterans who went to war
Later to come home, feeling depression
Who knows how it affected their children
Perhaps she's looking out for generations

Maybe it's for the engineers
Who built her schools
And the teachers
Who taught her
She won't let their hours spent, poured
Left unused without purposefulness
Protecting their children

Her alliance is all over
Not only her origin nation
Moving with empathy now a citizen American
Sprinkled with wisdom understanding
Thank god for the intuition
Lifting communities
From harmful productions
Or corruption

Emorruncy

The truth of reality is not only perception
Or even perspective

It's lived signals
Perhaps patterns or signs
Symbols in creation

Awareness beyond the senses
What do eyes really see?
Can one accurately perceive?

What mattered to each at 5 years of age
or 20
Even at 50
Who see's the mystery?

How high is each, in spirit essence?
Does one capsize with comparison?
Or throw darts, even bombs
In bars or wars

Oh wisdom understanding
Please grip all from doing the harming
Reminding them of soul connection

Slide Tides

Have you roamed above the terrain?
To see conscious manifestations in the open
Religious bodies interconnected
Are events dismissed as mundane incidents?
Or will one see through across the oceans
Deeper layers

Who here will put down identity?
Perhaps weapons to be superhuman
To see truth functions

Can't give the final answer
Root cause analysis
But here is a clue
Who is responsible, over who?
What's the alliance?
Who here truly has been a guardian?
Protecting
While the young develop with grace
Cultivating deeper understanding

Awareness won't fail you
Neither will the will
Better answer the call
Beyond all the buildings and skyscrapers

Realize

If only each took time
To seek understanding

If only each closed their eyes
To feel what's in the heart space

If only each sat under the tree
To appreciate the silence
Purity

If only each slowed down reactions
To observe how it all is functioning

If only each stood still
To not be swayed
Trusting intuition

Choosing
Valuing souls
Above deep pockets
Even if production can make things effective

Woving into the fabric, perhaps a bit
You know what I'm talking about?
Is it love or a reinforcement?
Distractions
Harmful consumption to later become a diagnosis

Better to have equilibrium

What's the pH?
Seventh heaven
Water currency
Replenishing sense making

If only, we can
Change
To hear those who are quiet
Instead of blaming it on parents

Why evaluate biased?
Perhaps now it's time to start believing
Instead of probabilistic algorithmic operations

Bold Action

Structured faith
Beyond the sun, stars, and the moon
Have any not passed the test?
To transcend beyond division

Have any weighed the representation?
A symbol of each culture and religion
Through continents
What do each reflect?
If not world function

How can any put others down?
And expect to be lifted beyond
What will each have to let go to glow?
Perhaps it's the dark that's keeping them

Deconstructing, not destructing or chaos full of lies
Open the arms, here comes the truth
"Souls are created equal"
It's true,
if the young, insecure, and vulnerable aren't exploited
And each aims to lean into accountability

Stimulant

Magnetic field
Cosmology
A force
Supporting

Who is willing to be selfless?
To put others feelings first
Who will rise higher?
Amidst the chaos and fighting
To see the emotional operation

Who speaks kindness when hated?
Who will give the shirt off their back to the homeless?

Who apologizes in accountability, without arrogance?
Who assumes in kindness before hasting into judgments?
Going the distance, to seek understanding

Who has felt the harm?
And decided to forgive regardless and be the change
Cultivating awareness

Who has been betrayed beyond imagination?
Who has shown up and give it all they've got,
even when others had cast spells and deceptions in operations
Blinding their ways

Who here has been broken open?
Just so others can find fortune

If not one of us, who is worthy?
To not be blind, to see clearly

Perhaps, still walking through it
Either what is or to be doing different
Not sure if any really are innocent

Mirror mirror on the wall
Who's the brightest of them all?
Mirror mirror on the wall
Can each see beyond the surface to others near
Winning with love and peace
Valuing honesty

Fracking Quackery

Development is a process
Did it not take months to labor?

Development takes time
Has she not put her life on the line?

Development takes energy
Has he not spent his days working?

Development shapes you
Has a community set truth healthy foundation

How developed is each origin?
Through the generations
Environment and priorities

Focused time and attention
Building truth shelter connection
Before the physical operation
And the population, thinks the mark of a true leader is influence
Rather than moral ethics

What has transpired or been transferred?
Who here will rise above to make the difference,
set aside their affluence to do right through actions

*Oh each is but a spec
In the timeline of space*

*Each is but a fingerprint
On this white canvas as big as the oceans
Who will have to sleep with their conscious*

*How will each beauty grow now, after the truth surfaces?
Will we continue to bury it?
Rather than investigate it*

*Operating in silos
Easier to have a paycheck
Buying ego fulfillment
Where is the heart richness?*

*Not sure if any will be able to see
Through the ripples
Seen and unseen
When all their concerned about is their own profits and security*

*Who's got blood on their hands?
Under their fingernails after spending days blaming it on the victims*

*You think the money of the wicked goes to the righteous
Little do you know, they've been trying to bury your neighbor*

*What was the law? If not love
Who here knows true function
While they give you the scalpel, "do what you please"
Feel indulgence cut you deep
While we watch you bleed*

<u>Jayed</u>

How will you know something is good for you?
Especially when you've been conditioned to consume hurting

How can you trust the different?
It seems so foreign

How can you have faith in another?
When it doesn't mix with inner narrative?

This author isn't out to deceive
Oh my
Oh my
Out of billions
Even gazillions through history
One deciding to uplift

Even when it almost pulled her into the darkness
That can devour

She's reaching for you with love
To get you above it

Trying to pull you out of that mess
Even hurt feelings
Even the lies, based on dependence for modeled business operations

Oh my the whole globe she's asking for
To move from harm and chaos into the sacred

Don't fear
Angels are with her
Not the one's pretending to be
But those in the seen and unseen
Little does she know, you too
Never alone
A whole army
Given life
To bring about meaningful change

So why hate or over generalize the foreigners, why?
Some didn't even know how to do harm, until they arrived
At times, can be taught new ways, to build this beautiful space
Being more welcoming
Instead of being targeted

Can you feel the tides, changing?
To have soulful connection
New thinking
To elevate nations
Changing generations
For peaceful becoming
Or is each still concerned, "How can I raise my net worth"
Rather than valuing the truth

The Upright Don't Fight

It's easy to be subjective about it all
Comparing the world to your essence

It's the easiest to compare to the trees and what can be seen
Mirror neurons rather than empathy

It's easy to glance up and down in envy
Operating in lifestyle
Feeling famous
Until one realizes they're using a person as an object to make profit

But where and who has courage?
To know their faith can make all the difference
Braving and enduring

Who has love on the inside?
Looking out for their neighbors

Who can put their pride aside?
For one more moment, one more try,
ask for true guidance from heaven
To heal the soul of a nation
Without violence

Who will do it?
The impossible
Making it possible
Be of good moral character
Leading with love being an example
So we can change the tides, perhaps if not for ourselves
The next generation

<u>Superb Symphony</u>

Yea, yea
Isn't it always something
Fighting before evaluating

Yea, yea
Who's there?
Another one pointing a finger

Yea, yea
Brave path
Who here is willing to do different?

Yea, yea
A new tune
Who will change from the inside to experience the truth?

Yea, yea
It might hurt at first
When all the lies that have been told burn

Yea, yea
Boom bloom
Look now
New vision

Not value of disturbance or destruction
Better peaceful radiant essence 'us'

Don't take a path or follow anyone
Not even her
Better make sure you're not under influence
People or products
Even emotions that can have you blindly consuming

Don't you remember?
Look above
Or inside
See
Perhaps not with your eyes but spirit
Learning
Maybe it's the limbic system

Who are you following?
Is it just or justifying?

One that doesn't speak ill intentions
But reinforces forgiveness
Into kindness
Without blame
Sharing understanding
Encouraging accountability
A little more empathy

<u>Beyond the Veil</u>

The gifts endowed aren't world given
They're tools that help give soul enrichment

A smile that brightens another's day
A hand that builds shelter

Even the biggest muscle
Speaking, truth caring
Don't blame it on Karen

That's it, you know it
It's in the making
A new movement

How will each exercise their gifts?
The hand or touch
Either in the physical or perception
Or the tongue that keeps talking

How will each win the hearts?
Not keeping trophies and glory from the sickness,
leading to harm conditioning

Oh the subconscious is tricky
When one speaks, another interprets
To keep operating, modeling, even when it's hurting

Be it ego or soul?
Check with the heart, you'll know
Is it yours or the people?
Feedback being heard is important

Reviews online, sure those could be engineered
But what is being brought to light in the court and senate hearings?
Reverse root cause analysis

Index Record

Oh the shivers
Come with the glimmers
Not from the cold
But the glow

Not jumping into ice baths
But writing truths

The nerve
Appreciated
Oh, guess so
Not numbing
Choosing different

Why numb?
Why override the evidence?
The memories surfacing, surfing
Solving the riddle

EMDR, really?
Why investigate the memory, without emotions
Objective review of evidence processing
Forensic analysis

Why reach out to the physical?
When you've got a clear conscious
Can see it different

It won't even hurt to face any of it
What hurts is running from it

So, sit still
Under a tree
Journal and identify consumption inventory

Sit
And start doing, others will too
Slowly all that harm will come undone
No longer populating

Sit
Be still
Breathe, if you feel any pain
And trust, the process of change

In the chippers of the silence
And the wind
Being and covering
Those who were exploited

Sit
Don't run
Come under the tree
Be freed
Beyond the world
And dark imaginings

Companion

Every little one has run with the wind
Even against it
At times, falling to their knees

Little ones climbing up
Even through the obstacle course

And one day comes
You realize
Little ones are grown

What has become of each one?
In the eyes of their parents

They were put to the tests, time and time again
At school or even the open

But each parent has had to let go and move with faith
Hoping other parents will be kind to their young ones,
when they find them

Each parent, trusting their little ones
Because they taught them, right from wrong and guidance

*But boy oh boy,
this world is tempting*

*Lord knows, it is
Even packaged with feels in news feeds
A suggestive reinforcement
Stealing attention*

*It's okay
The world serves it's purpose
Strengthening you from within
And reminding you, to trust soul essence instead*

*Little ones are you still little?
Even when you're older*

*Are you brave to answer your calling?
And bring out loving healing*

*Paving a path
Beyond understanding
To help and develop kindness*

*Hooray!
What a change
Rocked you back and forth since the day you were born*

Originality

Before the walkers for the elders
Were men and women who helped them

Before innovation
How much did each lean?
On another other out here
Without guilt but patience

If one had fallen
How many ran to them
Lifted them up, without condescends

If this is a game
Who here is a good sport?
Or are we lost in the racism?
Still acting like children, pointing the fingers

"Mommy daddy, did you see?
Their skin and behaviors don't look like me"

Perhaps, some are still feeling it
The training
Veered to only see skin tones
Not hear the music of truth
Through empathy
Asking better questions

Hero Win

*She's going the other way
Not into the chaos*

*She's growing in other ways
Pouring kindness and sharing wisdom*

*She's taking another route
Not mimicking what's presented
Asking questions*

*She's moving different
Yes, she is, into the sacred*

Oh, you want to know why?

*Well...
Can't you see heaven?
About to be built
New vision*

*Perhaps starting with the pages into those near
Building foundation in hearts and mental temples*

*Or reaching out to the orphans,
who may be struggling
Reminding them,
don't consume the poison or seek false belonging
Trust intuition
Won't leave you feeling broken*

Act with Love, Better Help

Everything changes
There are cycles
Are you in a loop, feeling like a broken record?
or bringing out the truth to change the tides
Without wine or complaints

Sparking new states
Beyond the blue and red nationals
Everything changes

Growth
And there will come a time to do different

Here, is a carved path
Full of hope and love
To up above

You want to feel the truth don't you?
Perhaps more of the same, can ego fulfill you

But tell me,
is what your experiencing evolving civilization?
Or are you more concerned about spirit conversions?

Have you walked through the experience yet?
Or do you have a blind spot because of proximity
Perhaps the best interest of the lobbyist

<u>Blueberry Muffin</u>

You feel alone?
There's another near you
Not physically
Perhaps an angel

That see's all your true attributes
Even your walk
At times, you have even looked dazed because of yesterdays

There's one that see's you wholesome
Beyond identity as your true self

There's plenty of us out here
Who see your true essence
Beyond the identity, world operation

There are others who agree with this message
Soul radiance

They often say, birds of a feather flock together
But who are the angels?
Where are they?

*Lets see who show's up with love
To start a loving change
Not throwing tantrums
But sitting in stillness
Moving with peaceful essence
Or is history going to repeat itself?*

*Ghandi, how did you do it?
Do we need to fast and sit with peace to make changes?
In perception putting down all idols
Choosing to show up and look beyond the horizons*

*No one upholding themselves as anything full of arrogance
But extending and opening a hand to meet a new friend
Sharing their story
Putting it all in perspective*

*Even if you're alone while reading this
Know, pretty soon
There will come a time
A new opportunity carved out
To lead with love
In this generation or the other*

*Each has that power
To be a beacon of light beyond understanding
Instead of blaming and character assassinating
Leaning into cultivating accountability
Honor of fellowship*

Sweet Honeycomb

Oh love can make you tremble
Just like fear
But love is different because it heals

Not comparing or contrasting
Sharing meals

Love picks you up
Calls you up

Fear can pull you down
Whispering in your ear, to tell lies
With a dark perception

Better listen to surface intuition

Love reaches through the horizons
To lift with new chances
While fear can have you spinning in,
false opinions

Love touches all, without confusion
Pouring clarity
While fear charges for outcomes, sentencing

It's funny because
Love and fear are the same coin
Except, one values the truth
Seeks understanding

Love, don't be scared
Why is fear gripping you?
Fear is there for a reason, only to strengthen
Playing it's part, a role as a spec
In this beautiful story
Humanity

There comes a time,
when each of us will have to let the fear go
To grow
Beyond the horizons
Forever more
Everlasting

Leaving a light on
For those who may be hurting

Fear not love, love is here
Love, loving and living out the fear
You do belong here

Physically sure, but be more so in the heart
Even when you change nothing of your physical,
you're accepted
Embodying kindness and love

<u>Bonjur</u>

Hope, here it is
Look how much resides here

Hope, what a dear friend
Even when the dark exists

Hope, she shines
Beyond the baselines

Hope sets new standards
And calls
To the ones beside her
"Come look, new vision"

Hope is a name
We can all write it into our wirement
On the end of our fingerprint

Hope, oh my you're everywhere
Even around those reading this

Breathing, through
Hope we'll never forget you

Better Belief

What if I fall?
Yea, that would be hard
But like birds,
your instincts will kick-in
And wings will break open

Here soaring

You can make a difference

Through each scene
Believe
Believe
Believe
You can grow beyond the fears
To help and be good to others near

Even if you've made mistakes
Writing the wrongs can have the power
To change the tides
For a better future

Relief

How delicious?
This is
It's a little spicy
But even cayenne pepper adds to the mix
Better strength
Not human traffic

Oh the spice
Not like fine wine
Keeping those beauties under harm

Spicy
The truth
Moving out of buried worlds

Is it red or is it blue?
Spicy life
Not fueling to hate
Only pulling others out of feels
To better awareness to see

Oh the spice
Live life
Wisdom and fortune of intuition
Better make sure
You are not blinded by consumption
Weigh the variables
Feel empowered to ask questions

Huey of Que Heuristics

Oh being legendary
Perhaps holographic
Shinny
Collectibles
Rising above senselessness

It's not about any one subjectively
To get famous or glory

Oh it's not about anything each can have
It's all about what is being poured out

So what do you fill in your cup?
And those of others?

Feel love and shared change
It's possible to be a winner in this space
Not individually, can you hear unity?

When one wins from source, all will have fortunes
Truth Guidance
So they or children don't burn in the fire
As the brave lead through the uncharted

<u>Lucky Gem</u>

*The arcades are there early on
For the children to play in competition
As the young develop
Going to established environments
Mirror neurons or DDR?
Later to mimic the screen presentation*

*What about the casinos?
777
Are you truly a winner?
Or being conditioned
Better yet, lets ask, "Who developed it?"*

*Is the gambling truth norm?
If not all that money is spent on education
Later developing new DNA engineered genetics*

*Even dancing in schools
Leading to mistress moves
By those who think it's truth norms
To later take off their spiritual robes
As they mimic environmental identity operation*

Do the products we sell on the shelf
Drain into the sewage to later be consumed
Then others blame it on the government
When no one is really weighing the variables

How has a dollar affected emotions
Into operations
From their childhoods

Who asks questions here?
Who?
Seeks deeper understanding before pointing their finger

To wonder and not wander,
how is each product affecting or dissolving
Instead of revolting

Have we weighed the variables?
Or do we just keep producing
Even if its poison
Lobbying
Moral turpitude understanding

It's alright
It's okay
Here these heavenly ones coming to make a change

<u>Goldhood Robinhood</u>

*You can say each is guilty all you want
They are guilty in perceptions*

*Sure all will be guilty as identified
But who here is wise?*

*Seeing past behaviors
Hidden layers
Perhaps through time
Space
Even coherence
Sound waves, currency*

*If you are feeling the guilt, be freed
You are not at fault here*

*Remorse is important
But even more so, rising above it
Building new mending understanding
So others are not hurt or harming*

*Be inspired
We need you! We really do!*

*Take inspired action
Don't let impulsivity or craving sink the fortress
Even in mental functions
Build to roam in heavenly castles
In perception, anything is possible
To get those who have felt down into paradise understanding*

<u>Taxonomy Mommy</u>

The sky is so far
Have you seen it?
Even when you traveled through it

Perhaps, you're already beyond the horizons if you can perceive
I've taken you there
This is true
With truth
Seeing across the plane, above the terrain
Without violence
If this is not love, what is?

Some build the shuttles and the ships
While another one chooses temples

How can we build what is on the outside?
If we did not take time to check with our heart posture?

After you finish this, know you'll start doing different
And pretty soon, you'll see yourself rising
To feel and fuel love
Building a new home

Perhaps not over anyone, just thyself
Winning true fortunes
Feeling better
With compassion

Harmalytics

The call may find you when you barely have it together
Amidst perplexity wondering
What will you choose in the open?
While everyone around is in indulgence

The call is so backwards, turning the dial
Powerful and intuitive
Exposing truths
Not worshiping false idols

The call is hard and sweet
Like a dear friend whispering,
"hurt is not true experience"

The call will give guidance
The one in a million
Not sure how many you will get
But if you get called
Answer with strength

You've got a well of courage
And an angel who will uplift
Don't doubt the soul essence

<u>Positive Force</u>

This poetry isn't about breakups
A buildup
It started as a diary, written to help others

This poetry is set with intention to elevate understanding
With pure intentions to raise awareness

How powerful is that?
To not seek selfishness from the tribe
It matters how each treats and treads
Being gentle

Is this sweet or perhaps with time can make all the difference
Good Gracious

Can't we see the potential? An overcoming

Even when one has walked in harm because of all that was established
A lifestyle scoped to operate in a certain way
To feel belonging
Or is it group thinking?

At times, reflecting "is it our fault?"
To only understand, others may be following programming
Neocortex
A brain function or admiration
Perhaps, it's just emotions

Gotta smile about it
Or that frown might stick
Carrots and sticks
Rewards or punishments
Oh here we go again, back to reinforcement
No wonder we keep cycling

Twin Power

If it wasn't for 'the one'
The future could have faced a different trajectory
So remember to be thankful
Memorials in silence

If it wasn't for 'the one'
Looking, sharing flowers being a guardian
Who knows what would have happened
Outcome bias

Each can grow
Away from falsehood perceptions
Also is a poison

Required to lead with compassion
Understanding
Valuing the making

So pay respects,
take a moment to be silent
Instead of gossiping or revolting
Building life
Not only for thyself
But collective

If you even to try to come after this author for this spoken
You will feel how far you stand
Way beneath, in the underground

Orchid Paradise

All the hours spent
Time investment of all those who poured into it

The love given is never lost
All the hours invested
Won't be spent in the hurting

The encouragement and second changes, with chances
As all develop in radiance
Won't be wasted
In time or attention
Because it's made about prep pills or digital apps

What's life like for kids to be playing in the backyards?
Are they still selling trampolines?
To study gravity or magnetism
Who is aiming to be intelligent?

At times, the hurt can reside
Under the surface
Covering the eyes with tears
Subconscious operations
That misguide the young and vulnerable early on
What's up with the chat rooms?
Or the plasma donations
Come to think about it, who is the vampire?
Sucking other's blood for a dollar

Here comes the love
Picking up your chin whispering,
"The love is never lost or forgotten.
We are love, so feel inspired to seek understanding"

All this time
Past days
Not passing out

Time spent and burned
Like calories, not self consumed

Love won't fail
It's impossible
Sure ain't
Here look
This smile
And the crowned, with a sword of love
To cut the chains
Sharing glimpses of what's occurring

Others matter just as much as you do

Or did they not tell you?
Those who truly lead, find it in their heart to have empathy
Instead of casting judgments
Identifying duress function

Hood Mysteries

You should have seen them
In fetal position
Crying

Oh hurt processed in childhood

But there will come a time
Trust
When you will have to bloom
Not in tears

At first you'll run around
So much energy
Lifefull gift given
Through shock electricity

Embracing the seasons
Picking up your love weapon
Never falling
To the misguides of who show up telling you nonsense
Proposing offers for better money if you do pornography
When there are grants offered to those established businesses
Feeding and breeding falsehoods
Reinforcing harm productions

En Banc Review

This writer didn't ever think she was going to be an author
Poetry in a technological era
When everyone has phones reading propaganda
So humorous

You can grow up all your days, other's asking you
"What will you become? Which profession will you choose?"
Is it truth?

Her mother wanted her to be a doctor
But perhaps god had better plans,
knowing what brings this place true healing
Perhaps awarness

Better than a light
Leaving goodness
Leading out in the open to lift others through perceptions
Even if its spicy
We need to understand how this will guide
Not just about us
Taking a hit for the greater good

There's no way anyone could have predicted this
Trust, she's just as perplexed
Is it possible?
Even the weirdest can be from the highest?

No one is weird or a nerd
There is no world classification that can ever define you

You are beyond beyond beyond
Soul glowing radiance

The spirit of all people love,
not against
Even if they misbehaved in the open

There is a place for you
As big as you can perceive
Full of loving feels
And nourishment in ways unseen

You're never alone
Don't feel scared
We're all here for a reason and purpose
To brighten this beautiful space

So, feel inspired to be a lighthouse here
Leading with curiosity
Cultivating awareness
Like sweet honeycomb and blueberry muffins

<u>Justice League</u>

How can this help?
Out in the infrastructure

Perhaps gauging what derives, hurt becoming

Why build others temples?
Will it really make a difference?
Guiding others to choose different
Weighing the variables
Instead of propagating criminals
Or even distrust
Because of what's out in the open, cycling
To be buying all the toilet paper in fear

How will a girl change anything?
Girl power
Figuring out the capability of root cause analysis

If one can be manipulated into harm
Perhaps, using perceptions to lift can do the trick
Therefore anything is possible
Beyond logic understanding

How will each now choose?
To grow with intention
Being prudent and truthful
Shifting the focus to true soul essence

*Perhaps empathy
Not one in uniform putting up defenses*

*Perhaps compassion to understand the needs
Of the physical, social, economical and the feels*

*Trust as you read, there will be plenty who decide
Choosing different, hey!
Can make all the difference*

*Not operating in certain identities to amplify energies
Group thinking
When it may be leading you to a dead ending*

*Sharing a lens, alternate perspective
To bridge understanding
So others are not hurting
Leading for outcomes full of joy
Hope too*

Remember, don't let that which you consume, consume you

New Path

Does it end here?
Or is this the beginning?
Do we run? Or rise becoming true ones?

Will we ask deeper questions?
Derive better solutions
Or will we roll our eyes
Looking down on others because of what they have
When they bought what they could with offered wage

Perhaps a better conditioning in awareness
To assume kinder, looking into their heart space

Or will the gold be hidden
Do we have to keep fiddling in the mud and dark
To find the true gems
Who were right in front of us

What is true luxury?
In the eyes who see
Is it in material or shared experience wisdom
To give comprehension not depression

What is the truth north worth?
Who is fortunate?
To give a return on investment
Better than a hurtful becoming
Taking accountability

Perhaps its none of us
This could be a tragedy

Or
Or

There is HOPE

It can be one of us
That can lead with kindness
Cultivating awareness
Before pointing a finger, pausing, leaning into curiosity

The power isn't outside of you
Nope
Giving it back
You've got soul power, choosing different

Here comes freedom
Packaged as a new one
Perhaps it's a foreigner
Serving the justice
A little spicy and sweeter

Perhaps, it's victory for the people!

-smiles-

"America will never be destroyed from the outside.
If we falter and lose our freedoms,
it will be because we destroyed ourselves."

- Abraham Lincoln

Book soundtrack:
Fortitude - Lance Conrad

About the Author

Farah Alqattan has continued her legacy writing 'To you From you' by sharing the fifth and final installment, 'Proof is in the Pudding'. This book was written Summer of 2024 with the help of forces unseen. She aimed to publish 'Proof is in the Pudding' to inspire others to cultivate awareness while leading with empathy, kindness, and compassion.

As she blooms again, Farah shows the readers the power of perception and the possibilities of leveraging experience for good while carving an opportunity for meaningful change for persons and communities. We hope you enjoyed this, feel encouraged to share the publications with anyone who may need it.

About the Publisher

Rwh Publishing LLC was established in 2023 to publish creative content by artists that aim to uplift humanity and change lives for the better. If you would like to support, share this with those who need it.

Thank you!

www.ingramcontent.com/pod-product-compliance
Lightning Source LLC
Chambersburg PA
CBHW020654060526
44119CB00069B/46